P9-DIZ-642

MONICA HALPERN

RAILROAD FEVER

Building the
Transcontinental Railroad
1830–1870

NATIONAL GEOGRAPHIC

Washington, D.C.

PICTURE CREDITS
Cover: Courtesy Central Pacific Railroad Photographic History Museum,
© 2003, CPRR.org; pages 1, 16, 18, 20, 26, 32, 34 The Granger
Collection, NY; pages 2-3, 5 (inset), 9-11, 23-25, 28, 33, 36-37 North
Wind Picture Archives; pages 4-5 © Scott T. Smith/CORBIS; pages 6-7,
9, 10, 11, 17, 23, 27, 33, 35, 37 © Todd Gipstein/CORBIS; pages 6-8,
17 Library of Congress; pages 11 (top), 12 (right), 13-15, 19, 29, 33
(inset) 38-39 Union Pacific Historical Collection; page 12 (left & 3rd
from left) Bancroft Library, University of California at Berkeley; pages
12 (2nd from left), 30-31, 35 Culver Pictures, Inc., NY; page 21
© Bettmann/CORBIS; page 22 Archive Photos, NY; page 27 Brown
Brothers, Sterling, PA; page 31 (inset) Hulton Getty Picture
Collection/Stone.

QUOTATIONS
Page 4 from Tracks Across America, by Leonard Everett Fisher (New
York: Holiday House, 1992), p. 39; page 8 from Hear That Lonesome
Whistle Blow, by Dee Brown (New York: Holt, Rinehart and
Winston,1977), p. 26; page 12 from "Mrs. Judah's Letter," the Bancroft
Library, U. C. Berkeley as quoted in Nothing Like It in the World, by
Stephen E. Ambrose (New York: Simon & Schuster, 2000), p. 59; page
15 from Nothing Like It in the World, p. 382; page 19 from A Work of
Giants: Building the First Transcontinental Railroad, by Wesley S.
Griswold, p. 92, as quoted in Nothing Like It in the World, pp. 164-65;
page 21 from How We Built the Union Pacific, by Grenville Dodge,
Washington, D.C., 1910, p. 31, as quoted in Full Steam Ahead: The
Race to Build a Transcontinental Railroad, by Rhoda Blumberg
(Washington, D.C.: National Geographic Society, 1996), p. 81; page 25
from My Early Travels and Adventures in America and Asia, by Henry
Morton Stanley, vol. 1, p. 211, as quoted in Nothing Like It in the
World, p. 266.

IBSN: 0-7922-6767-2

Library of Congress Cataloging-in-Publication Data

LC Control #2003017858
Complete CIP data available on request.

Table of Contents

"And the Iron Horse, the earth-shaker, the fire-breather . . . shall build an empire."

Ralph Waldo Emerson,
Poet and Philosopher

Settlement of the United States, 1850

CANADA

Oregon Country
Treaty with Britain 1846

Treaty with Britain 1818

Missouri River

Louisiana Purchase 1803

Treaty with Britain 1783

Original 13 Colonies

Treaty with Mexico 1848

PACIFIC OCEAN

ATLANTIC OCEAN

Texas 1845

Mississippi R.

MEXICO

Treaty with Spain 1819

N

Gulf of Mexico

0   500 mi
0   500 km

Introduction

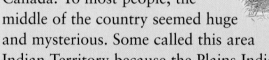

By the 1840s, the United States had been settled westward from the Atlantic Ocean as far as the Missouri River. Areas near the Gulf of Mexico and the Pacific Ocean were also settled. These areas included Mexico, the Texas Republic, Oregon Country, and British Canada. To most people, the middle of the country seemed huge and mysterious. Some called this area Indian Territory because the Plains Indians lived there. Others called the area the Great American Desert because they thought nothing would grow there.

Then, in 1848, gold was discovered in California. The promise of easy riches drew tens of thousands of people. Some traveled by ship around South America. Others traveled across the plains on horseback or in wagon trains. Some even walked! However they traveled, the journey was slow and dangerous. Those who made it to California found even more problems. Bringing supplies in and shipping gold out was hard, slow, and expensive. There were no roads. There were only rough trails.

For years, a few dreamers had been urging the building of a railroad connecting the Atlantic and Pacific coasts of North America. This is the story of how their dream became a reality.

CHAPTER 1

The Iron Horse

In 1800, the United States was a **rural** country. Most people never traveled far from their homes and villages. They grew or made just about everything they needed on their farms, or they traded with their neighbors. If they had to travel, they rode in horse-drawn carriages or wagons along dirt roads. Sometimes they traveled by boat. Traveling from place to place took a long time.

By 1825, the United States was beginning to **industrialize**. Factories were built. These factories needed **raw materials** to operate. They also had to get their finished products to customers. Cheaper, faster, and better ways of shipping materials and finished goods had to be found. The answer was the railroad.

During the 1700s, inventors developed the steam engine. This machine used steam to do such work as turning wheels, grinding grain, or sawing wood. In 1800, a mechanic in England had the idea of attaching a steam engine to a carriage. This idea of a horseless carriage powered by an engine led to the development of the railroad.

Meet the *Tom Thumb*

In 1830, a New Yorker named Peter Cooper built the first locomotive in America. The engine was so small that it was named *Tom Thumb* after the storybook character. On its first trip, the locomotive was challenged to a race with a horse-drawn carriage. The horse leapt away in the lead. The *Tom Thumb* quickly gained speed and passed it. The race seemed to be won! Suddenly, a piece of the locomotive's engine broke. The engine began to slow down. The horse won! But everyone could see what the locomotive could do.

Faster! Safer! Better!

In the 1830s, "railroad fever" hit America. It seemed as though every inventor was trying to build a better railroad.

Early rail travel was dirty, uncomfortable, and often dangerous. The open cars didn't protect passengers from bad weather. Sparks from the engine burned passengers' clothes and hair. Sometimes animals strayed onto the tracks, causing accidents. Brakemen on each car of the train had to apply the brakes by hand. So, stopping was a problem. Rail cars often tipped over when going around curves.

American engineers tried to solve these problems. They added a cowcatcher to the front of the engine. They also added a whistle and a lantern to let animals and people know the train was coming. Spark arresters on smokestacks reduced the risk of fire. Other inventions improved the railroad's safety, comfort, and speed. The railroad industry grew rapidly.

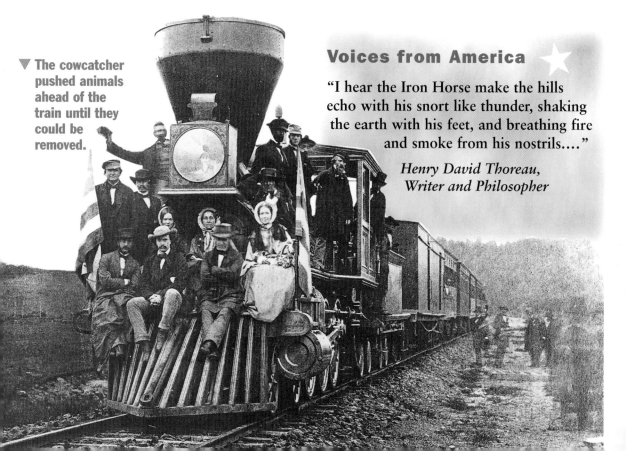

▼ The cowcatcher pushed animals ahead of the train until they could be removed.

Voices from America

"I hear the Iron Horse make the hills echo with his snort like thunder, shaking the earth with his feet, and breathing fire and smoke from his nostrils...."

Henry David Thoreau,
Writer and Philosopher

Stop the Railroad!

By 1835, more than a thousand miles of track had been laid. Rail lines stretched across the eastern half of the United States. Not everyone was happy with the railroad.

Trains were noisy. They belched thick smoke and red-hot sparks. They frightened cattle grazing on farmland. They scared horses pulling carriages and wagons. Farmers didn't want trains crossing their land.

Stagecoach drivers, canal owners, and inn-keepers also objected to the railroad. They didn't want the competition. They were afraid they would lose business.

However, the railroad couldn't be stopped. Railroads made it easier and faster for people to visit friends and relatives. Goods could be shipped more quickly, easily, and cheaply. So, factories and stores grew up around the railroad. People moved to the railroad towns. Towns built along a railroad route grew rapidly.

The "Wrong" Side of the Tracks

The railroad created a "right" and a "wrong" side of the tracks. The wind usually blew the trains' black smoke in the same direction, over to the "wrong" side of the tracks. This became the cheap rent side, the side where factories were built and the poor lived. The "right" side was where expensive shops and fine homes were built.

Railroad Fever Grows

By 1852, there were 9,000 miles of railroad track in America. Most of the track was in the Northeast. Some was in the South.

By 1854, there were 15,675 miles of track. Now travelers could board a train in New York, arrive in Chicago, and take another train to Council Bluffs, Iowa, on the east bank of the Missouri River. That was the end of the line. To go farther west, travelers had to take a boat across the river. They continued the trip by ox-drawn wagon, stagecoach, horseback, river raft, or on foot. Their westward journey was slow, hard, and dangerous.

The West was growing. Many people wanted to move there to look for gold, to farm, or to start new businesses. They needed better transportation. Leaders in government and business talked about building a **transcontinental** railroad. But where? Northern politicians wanted it to take a northern route. Southern politicians wanted it to take a southern route. What would be the best route? Who would decide?

Disaster!

When railroads were new, there were many accidents. At first, trains moved so slowly that few people were badly hurt. As locomotives moved faster, accidents became more serious. In 1853, a Boston-bound train sped through an open drawbridge. The engineer didn't see the signal that the bridge was open. The locomotive, three passenger cars, and the baggage car fell into the river. Forty-six people died, and eighty others were injured. Afterwards, people demanded new safety rules.

CHAPTER 2

Getting Started

Ted Judah was a young, smart engineer. He had plenty of experience building railroads all over the East. He knew a transcontinental railroad could be built. To prove it, he spent weeks out in the western wilderness. There, he mapped a good route through the Sierra Nevada mountains. Now he needed to convince people that his plan was the right one. Then he had to raise the money to build the railroad.

Theodore D. Judah

11

Finding the Money

Judah persuaded four businessmen from California to supply the money to start up his railroad. The four men were called the "Big Four." They were Collis Huntington, Mark Hopkins, Charles Crocker, and Leland Stanford. The new railroad company was called the Central Pacific.

Collis Huntington and Mark Hopkins were partners in one of the biggest hardware stores in the West. Charles Crocker was the owner of a dry goods store. Leland Stanford ran a wholesale grocery business. These men had left the Northeast to seek their fortune in the California gold rush. They didn't find gold, but they did get rich selling supplies to the miners.

By the 1860s, the California gold rush was slowing down. New discoveries of gold and silver had been made in Nevada. Towns there were booming. The four businessmen wanted to do business in Nevada. Judah convinced them that his railroad would make that possible.

Voices from America

"Everything [Judah] did from the time he went to California to the day of his death was for the great continental Pacific railway. Time, money, brains, strength, body and soul were absorbed. . . . It used to be said 'Judah's Pacific Railroad crazy.'"

— *Anna Judah, Ted Judah's wife*

Collis Huntington

Leland Stanford

Mark Hopkins

Charles Crocker

Two Railroads Formed

The Big Four sent Ted Judah to Washington, D.C., to ask the government for land and money to build the new railroad. Judah was successful. President Abraham Lincoln signed the Pacific Railroad Act of 1862.

This Act set up two companies to build the transcontinental railroad. The Central Pacific Railroad Company would begin work in California. It would lay tracks east. The Union Pacific Railroad Company would start at the Missouri River. It would lay tracks west. Somewhere in the middle, the tracks would meet!

The Big Four wanted to celebrate the start of the Central Pacific's work. They held a **groundbreaking** ceremony on a muddy street in Sacramento, the capital of California, in early 1863. A brass band played. Leland Stanford spoke: "We may now look forward to the day when… the Pacific will be bound to the Atlantic by iron bonds."

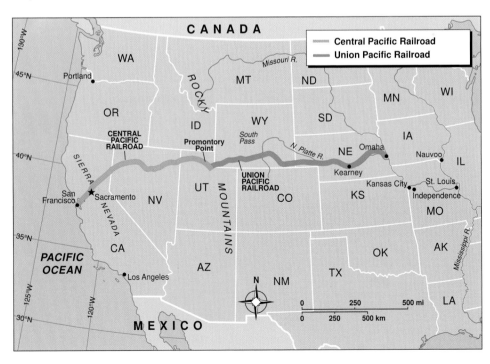

The Central Pacific Has Problems

Many miles of trackless mountains, deserts, and prairies lay between the two starting points. Judah had hoped to lay the first 50 miles of track in California by the fall of 1863, but progress for the Central Pacific was painfully slow. Workers were very hard to find. Men worked for a short time and then left for the Nevada mines.

Judah and the Big Four began to argue. Judah wanted to build the railroad slowly and carefully. The Big Four wanted to build it as fast as possible. They wanted to get rich. The sooner the railroad was built, the sooner they would get their money.

The Big Four won the fight. Furious, Judah sailed to New York to try to find other **investors**. On the way, he became ill with yellow fever and died. He was only 37 years old.

The Union Pacific Starts Up

The Union Pacific Railroad Company was run by a different kind of leader. Thomas Durant was a doctor, but he wanted to make lots of money. He thought that the Union Pacific could make him millions.

"Doc" Durant figured out that the companies that actually built the railroad would make the most money. So, he set up a construction company known as the Crédit Mobilier. Then he got the Union Pacific to agree to pay his company $50,000 per mile for laying the track. The actual cost would be about $30,000 per mile. The difference would go into Durant's pocket. This crooked scheme was but the first of many.

Voices from America

"So we admire those who did it— even if they were far from perfect— for what they were and what they accomplished and how much each of us owes them."

— *Stephen E. Ambrose, Writer*

Directors of the Union Pacific stand by a sign announcing that UP workers had laid 247 miles of track across Nebraska. ▼

Building the Union Pacific Line

In April 1865, the Civil War ended. The building of the Union Pacific could finally begin. By the spring of 1866, the **frontier** village of Omaha, Nebraska, had become the headquarters for construction. Building materials were shipped there. Workers began to pour into town looking for jobs.

The Union Pacific's job of building the railroad may have been harder than that of the Central Pacific. First of all, the Union Pacific had farther to go. For most of the western land it crossed, there were no maps. No one knew where the mountains, lakes, or rivers were. Also, Native Americans lived throughout the area. They hated the railroad because it crossed their hunting grounds and disturbed the buffalo. Sometimes, Native American war parties attacked railroad workers.

There were other problems. Much of the region had little wood or water. Wood was needed to make the railroad ties. The wood that was available was cottonwood, which was soft and rotted easily. So, hardwood and water had to be brought long distances to the railroad workers.

CHAPTER 3

The Workers

At its peak, there were over 30,000 workers building the transcontinental railroad. Finding those workers was very difficult. The Central Pacific hired workers, only to lose them to the gold and silver mines. The mines paid better.

Charles Crocker, one of the Big Four, became construction supervisor of the Central Pacific. He hired Irishman James Harvey Strobridge, known as "Stro," as his construction boss. Desperate for workers, Crocker suggested hiring Chinese. The Chinese would work for only $35 a month, much less than other workers earned. Stro turned down the idea. He thought the Chinese were not strong enough. He also thought other workers would refuse to work with them. But Crocker insisted. Finally, Stro agreed to try out 50 Chinese. After a month, Stro had to admit that the Chinese had done a great job. By the end of the year, there were 7,000 Chinese working on the railroad.

Blasting Forward

The Central Pacific Railroad had to cross the Sierra Nevada mountains. Many laughed at the idea! The Sierras cut California off from the rest of the country. They form an enormous ridge 400 miles long. Mountain peaks rise as high as 14,000 feet.

Nothing was going to stop the Central Pacific from moving forward. Workers drilled, blasted, built bridges, dug tunnels, and cleared forests. Work was painfully slow. Then Stro and his crew came to a wall of rock called "Cape Horn." Somehow the railroad track had to curve around the mountain. Hundreds of explosives had to be set off to blast the granite from the mountains and form a ledge for the track.

Engineers thought it couldn't be done. A Chinese foreman told Stro that the Chinese were good at this kind of work. After all, the Chinese had invented explosive powder. All they needed were reeds from San Francisco. Desperate, Stro ordered the reeds.

The Chinese Way

The Chinese wove the reeds into large baskets. Then a Chinese crew lowered Chinese workmen in the baskets down the cliffside. Swaying in the wind, each man drilled holes into the rock, added explosive powder, and lit a **fuse**. The worker was hauled up the cliffside quickly. He had only a few seconds to make it back up the cliff before the explosion. Most made it, but some didn't.

The Chinese workers insisted on following their own **customs**. They were divided into gangs of 12 to 20 men, each gang with its own headman and cook.

The Chinese also bought their own food. It was shipped in from Chinese merchants in San Francisco. The Chinese ate oysters, fish, fruits, vegetables, and very little meat. They drank only warm tea made with boiled water. Other workers drank water directly from streams and lakes. Many got sick. The Chinese stayed healthy.

The Chinese shared small tents. They took daily sponge baths and washed their clothes. In their spare time, they led quiet lives. They stayed away from the other workers. Most saved their money. Some later settled in California and raised families. Others returned to China.

Voices from America

"Without the Chinese it would have been impossible to complete the western portion of this great National highway."

—*Leland Stanford*

Cooks' assistants carried tea to Chinese workers all day long. ▶

19

Working for the Union Pacific

By the early spring of 1866, a flood of young men were traveling westward. They were looking for work. Some were **immigrants**— many Irish, some Germans and Swedes. Some were former slaves. Others were ex-soldiers. All of them gathered in Omaha to work for the Union Pacific. The work was steady and paid well, $2 or more a day.

Jack Casement was put in charge of laying the track for the Union Pacific. A former general in the army, "General Jack" was only five feet four inches tall. His brother Daniel, who joined him, was even shorter. They were both hard workers, called by some "the biggest little men you ever saw."

The Casement brothers set a goal of one mile of track per day. They offered each worker laying track a pound of tobacco if the goal was met. Later, they changed the goal to a mile and a half. The new reward was a raise in pay to $3 a day. Finally, they asked the men to lay two miles of track a day for $4. These rewards pushed the workers to lay track faster and faster.

The Work Train

Workers were rapidly laying track across the prairie. The shortage of workers, one of the Union Pacific's problems, had been solved. But there were many other problems. How could supplies be brought out to the work crews? How could the workmen be fed? Where would they sleep?

The Casement brothers came up with a solution. They invented the work train. They attached about a dozen cars to an engine. Each car had a different job. One car was filled with tools. One was a blacksmith shop where horseshoes could be made or repaired. Another car had rough dining tables and a kitchen. Still another had built-in bunks. Flatcars followed carrying rails, spikes, bolts, and other supplies. Herds of cattle moved along with the train. They supplied meat for the workmen.

Building a railroad was like moving an army across the countryside. Most of the workers had served in the army during the Civil War. They understood how to work and move as a unit. They were used to obeying orders.

Voices from America

"It was the best organized, best equipped and best disciplined workforce I have ever seen."

—*Grenville Dodge, Chief Engineer, Union Pacific*

A Day in the Life of a Railroad Worker

The men rose each morning at first light. They washed their hands and faces in a tin basin. They ate a big breakfast and began work. The work was backbreaking. The men worked under a burning sun as well as in bitter cold and snow.

At noon the workers had an hour to eat a heavy dinner. They had soup, fried or roast meat, potatoes, coffee, and sometimes pies or cakes. After the noon meal, they took naps or rested. Then they went back to work. They stopped work an hour before supper. This meal was less rushed. Afterwards, the men played games, talked, and sometimes sang before going to bed.

Room and board cost $5 per week. The men slept in bunk beds on one of the train cars. These cars held 78 bunks stacked in threes. In the summer, the men slept outside on top of trains. They rarely bathed and almost never washed their clothes. Most had long hair and beards or mustaches.

CHAPTER 4

The Wild West

The Union Pacific Railroad crossed land on the plains that was mostly wide-open spaces. Native Americans lived and hunted on these lands. Herds of buffalo and other wild animals roamed there. Traders and gold **prospectors** had crossed the plains, but they had built very few settlements. Most Americans thought the plains was a great desert.

Now the Union Pacific wanted settlers to move onto the plains. The railroad was being built to carry goods and passengers from place to place. Where would these goods and passengers come from?

The government had given the railroads enormous amounts of land. The railroads could make money by breaking up this land into small plots and selling them. To attract settlers, the railroads sent out posters describing the plains as rich and fertile. They urged people to buy land immediately. Once the railroad was completed, prices would go up.

The Native Americans

One group of people was not pleased to see railroad workers laying tracks across the plains. They were the Plains Indians. These tribes included the Sioux, Lakota, Arapaho, and Cheyenne. For years, politicians had been calling for Native Americans to be removed entirely from routes to the West. Some tribes had already been forced to move onto **reservations**. Reservations were areas of land that no one else wanted. They were far from the tribe's usual hunting grounds.

The Native Americans were angry at the way they were treated. They hated the Iron Horse. Snorting and whistling, the railroad scared away wild animals. And white settlements followed the railroad.

Native Americans had always depended on wide-open spaces for hunting. Their way of life was being destroyed. As soon as tracks were laid across Native American territory, war parties of Sioux, Cheyenne, and Arapaho began to attack workers building the railroad.

Attack!

One of the worst attacks was by a party of about 40 Cheyenne led by Chief Pawnee Killer. They attacked the Union Pacific, cutting telegraph wires and bending the rails. When a train hit the damaged rails, the engine overturned. Seven crew members were killed. Another freight train crashed into the wreck and also overturned. The conductor ran back along the track and stopped a third train just in time. The Cheyenne burned the overturned trains.

Voices from America

"We built iron roads, and you cannot stop the locomotive any more than you can stop the sun or the moon."

—*General William T. Sherman,*
Army Commander

Railroad workers feared for their lives. Railroad owners, politicians, and military men wanted to crush the Native Americans. Troops went after them. Soldiers attacked both Native American war parties and peaceful settlements.

Finally, a Peace Commission was called. The generals told the Native Americans that they must let the railroad be built. Chief Pawnee Killer left the meeting in a rage. The Sioux and the Cheyenne continued their raids.

The Buffalo

The Plains Indians had another reason for hating the railroad. It split the Great Plains buffalo herd into two parts.

The Plains Indians depended on the buffalo for most of the things they needed. They ate the meat, both fresh and dried. They used the hides for clothing, tents, and ropes. They made tools and weapons out of the bones. They made thread, glue, cups, and spoons from the buffalo.

Buffalo skins became very popular with city people back East. The skins were used for clothes, blankets, carriage covers, and sleigh seats. Hunting buffalo became popular. The railroad held sight-seeing trips that included buffalo hunts. Passengers shot at buffalo from the windows of a moving train.

The railroads wanted to get rid of the buffalo. The animals damaged tracks. They used telegraph poles as scratching posts, knocking them over. If there were no more buffalo, the Native Americans would have to move away.

CHAPTER 5

The Great Race

In 1866, the government officially approved a race between the Central Pacific and the Union Pacific railroads. The Central Pacific was to build as fast as possible eastward. The Union Pacific was to build as fast as possible westward. The company that got the farthest would make the most money.

By the end of 1867, the Union Pacific was 540 miles west of Omaha. Their workers had laid 240 miles of track since January. Over the same period, the Central Pacific had laid only 40 miles of track. Their workers had to dig through the solid rock of the Sierras. They had to work through snowstorms. They had to avoid mud slides and **avalanches**. For months, the mostly Chinese workers worked in round-the-clock shifts seven days a week.

Which railroad would win? Newspapers all over the country wrote daily about the "great race." They printed the number of miles of track laid each day. Readers followed these reports with growing excitement. They felt like sports fans following a race for the championship.

Snow!

The winter of 1865–1866 saw constant rain and snow in the mountains of California. Mud slides and avalanches often blocked the tracks. The next winter was even worse. There were 44 snowstorms! Some dropped more than ten feet of snow.

Central Pacific workers did nothing but shovel snow away from the track roadbeds. Frequent snowslides buried the workers' camps. Some men froze to death. Bodies were sometimes not found until the spring thaw. Work was painfully slow, a gain of only a few feet a day.

Thirteen tunnels were drilled through the Sierra Nevada mountains during this period. Some were large enough for a team of horses to walk through. Here the workers lived, always in the dark. Only chimneys and air shafts poked out into the open air.

The heavy snows were costing the Central Pacific time and money. The directors finally decided to invest in an expensive improvement—snowsheds. These were roofs built over the track. Called "the Longest House in the World," these snowsheds covered 37 miles. They freed men to lay track instead of remove snow.

In the Desert

By 1868, the Central Pacific had finally dug its way out of the mountains. It had taken three years to cut through the Sierra Nevadas. At last the men were beginning to lay track on the flat Nevada desert. To have a chance to win the Great Race, the Central Pacific needed to move quickly. But there were new problems.

The path across the desert stretched nearly a hundred miles. There was no water. There were no trees and no building stones. Water and supplies had to be shipped long distances.

Also, the work gangs were entering the land of the Shoshone and Paiute tribes. Officials of the Central Pacific wanted peace with the Native Americans. They had learned from the Union Pacific's troubles. Central Pacific officials met with the tribal chiefs. They offered them free passage on the railroad. The chiefs could ride in the passenger cars. Other Native Americans could ride for free in the freight cars.

The Central Pacific also hired male and female Native Americans to work on the railroad. The women turned out to be good at using crowbars and sledgehammers. With their problems under control, the Central Pacific was able to build a mile or more of track per day. The race continued.

Boomtowns

As the railroads were built, towns grew up overnight along their path. People lived and worked in tents or shacks. These **boomtowns** existed for a short time. Railroad workers spent their free time and extra money there. The towns were rough places. Fights were common. Sometimes, men were killed. Once the railroad moved on, most towns disappeared.

Benton, Wyoming, was one such boomtown. It was located in the middle of the desert. Water had to be carried in by wagon from a river three miles away. No one washed. Most everyone and everything was covered with dust. Just about every day someone was murdered. When the railroad workers moved on after just two months, Benton was deserted. Nothing was left but a few broken-down shacks and a cemetery.

▼ Promontory, Utah

The Ten-Mile Day

The Central Pacific and the Union Pacific competed each day to see who could lay the most track. One day, the Central Pacific lay a bit more than six miles of track. On another day, the Union Pacific team began work at 3 A.M. and lay more than eight miles of track. Finally, Charles Crocker, the construction supervisor for the Central Pacific, announced that his men would lay ten miles of track in one day!

Crocker planned this day like a military operation. On April 28, 1869, as the sun rose, Chinese workers moved the iron forward. A hand-picked crew of eight Irish track layers began work. They had been promised four days' pay for the one day of work. Each man lay track as fast as he could walk.

By noon, six miles of track had been laid. The workers took their full hour for a relaxed meal. They were offered the chance to quit for the day while others took their place. But the proud men insisted on completing the job. By 7 P.M. that evening, they had laid 10 miles and 56 feet of track!

In one day, Central Pacific workers laid 10 miles and 56 feet of rail. This record was never broken. ▼

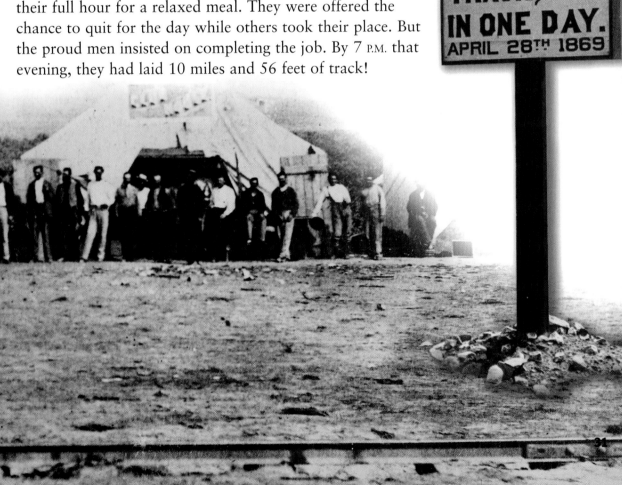

31

The Last Rail Is Laid

By the end of 1868, the two railroads were less than 400 miles apart. People had expected the transcontinental railroad to be completed in 1876, the 100th anniversary of the nation's birth. Instead, the railroad would be joined in 1869, seven years early!

The two companies finally agreed on a date and place of meeting: Promontory Point, Utah, May 10, 1869. The date and place had been set far enough ahead so that officials could arrive in time to take part in the ceremonies. The Central Pacific finished first, on April 30.

The big day arrived. The weather was perfect. Hundreds of people gathered around the two-rail gap. A huge American flag flew nearby. Chinese workmen carried one last rail. An Irish crew carried the other one. Everything was ready except the final spikes that fastened the rail to the wooden ties. Several bands played. The crowd cheered, and the last rail was laid.

Across the United States, people celebrated. In San Francisco, people in the streets celebrated late into the night. In Chicago, a parade seven miles long wound through the streets. In New York, a hundred guns were fired off.

▲ "Doc" Durant and Leland Stanford drove in a golden spike and joined together the Central Pacific and Union Pacific railroads.

CHAPTER 6

Riding the Transcontinental Railroad

ess than a week after the joining of the two railroads, train service began. Now, a person could travel from New York to San Francisco in seven days. By June 1870, the cost was $136 for a first-class ticket, $110 for coach, and $65 for third-class. The same trip used to take months and cost more than $1,000.

The cost of shipping goods by railroad was also much less than it had been. Mail sent across the country took only a few days instead of weeks to arrive and cost pennies instead of dollars.

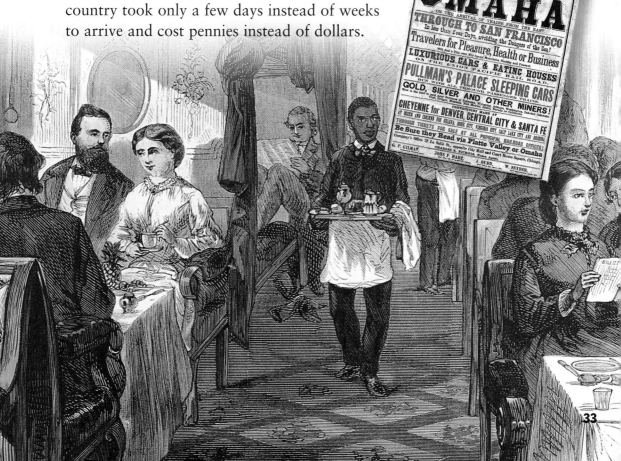

First-Class Travel

The rich wanted to experience the exciting "Wild West" they had only read about. They wanted to see the magnificent Western scenery described in the many new travel guidebooks.

First-class passengers on the railroad traveled in deluxe sleeping cars called Pullmans. Hinged beds could be let down at night and pulled up out of the way in the morning. Dining cars were richly decorated with velvet curtains and crystal chandeliers. Pullman chefs and waiters cooked and served delicious meals.

Travelers enjoyed watching the wildlife along the tracks. The weather entertained passengers, too. Violent thunderstorms, heavy, fierce blizzards, hailstorms, and tornadoes were all possible. Heavy rains were likely to flood the tracks. Hailstorms broke train windows. Tornadoes could lift a train off the track. Cross-country travel was often very exciting!

Passengers wait in an early railroad station. ▼

Immigrants Take the Train

Immigrants traveled on the new railroad, too. They were leaving the crowded cities in the East to find a better life in the West. They traveled in what were called Zulu cars. The passengers sat crowded together on hard benches. Each car had a stove for cooking and a toilet. There were no beds. People slept on the floor or in the aisles.

When the train stopped, passengers with extra money could buy a restaurant meal. Otherwise, people carried food with them or bought food at stops. The train stopped to load freight and mail, take on water, and allow passengers to stretch their legs.

Women and children sat in the last passenger cars, considered the safest in case of a head-on collision. Men sat in the middle cars. Sometimes, Chinese workers were on board. They were forced to sit in a separate car just behind the locomotive. Native Americans had to travel on the platforms outside the passenger cars or in the freight cars.

Meet the Pullman Porters

The first Pullman cars were staffed with newly freed African Americans. These men had worked on the plantations of the South as slaves. Now, they had no jobs. They grabbed the chance to work for pay, even low pay. They welcomed passengers, carried luggage, made up beds, and served food. For more than 100 years, Pullman porters were almost all African American.

Life on the Transcontinental Railroad

The trip across the country was sometimes boring. Travelers found ways to entertain themselves. Some read, talked to the other passengers, or played games. During the day, passengers stood on the platforms to look at the passing scenery. On Sundays, they could attend religious services.

As the train got farther west, the people who boarded were rougher. Some were described as hairy and unwashed. Many of the men chewed tobacco. They spit tobacco juice into brass containers called spittoons.

Some Pullman cars had organs. ▼

Sometimes, the train stopped at dining stations. The passengers were allowed off for 30 minutes to eat a meal. Most eating houses were wooden buildings filled with long tables. Large platters of food were set out for the passengers. Meal prices were usually one dollar.

Train Robbers

Only 18 months after the transcontinental railroad was completed, the first train robbers held up the train. Late one night, a gang of six climbed aboard an eastbound Central Pacific train. The train was carrying an enormous **payroll** of $40,000 for Nevada miners. The robbers demanded that the crew stop the train. Then they grabbed the money and escaped. Twenty-four hours later, the same train was held up by a different gang.

Jesse James and his brothers were the train robbers travelers most feared. The first train that the gang robbed was traveling across Iowa. The James boys tore up the track, causing the train to fall over on its side. Then the bandits appeared, demanding passengers' jewelry and money. The brothers leapt onto their horses and rode away.

The railroads hired armed guards to protect any train carrying a lot of money or valuables. Even so, holdups continued for many years.

What Changes Did the Railroad Bring?

The building of the transcontinental railroad forever changed the landscape of America. It also changed lives. Most Indian tribes lost their battle to hold onto their lands. They were forced onto reservations. Many immigrants who had helped build the railroad used their earnings to buy farmland from the railroads and settle the Great Plains.

Villages, towns, and cities grew up around train lines. Industries developed. The railroad brought valuable lumber and minerals from the West to factories in the East. Factories shipped their products by rail to customers quickly and cheaply.

The railroad even changed time. The trains needed reliable schedules. But every city, town, and village operated on its own time. They called it local or sun time. If it were 12 noon in one town, it might be 12:30 in a town a mile away. The railroads set up time zones across the country that followed the sun. Called "standard time," these time zones made railroad schedules work.

The building of the transcontinental railroad was one of the greatest achievements of the American people in the 1800s. It united the country from "sea to shining sea" and set the stage for a time of great growth.

Glossary

avalanche a fall or slide of a large amount of snow, ice, or earth down a mountainside

boomtown a town having a sudden rise in population

custom practice followed by a particular group

excursion a short trip made for pleasure

frontier the far edge of a country where few people live

fuse a cord that is lighted at one end to cause an explosion at the other end

groundbreaking the act of breaking ground to begin a construction project

immigrant a person who leaves one country to settle permanently in another

industrialize to set up businesses and factories

investor a person who gives or lends money to something, such as a company, in order to get more money back in the future

payroll the total of all money paid to workers

prospector a person who explores an area looking for gold, silver, or other valuable resources

raw material a substance in its natural state that is treated or processed and made into useful finished products

reservation an area of land set aside by the government for a special purpose

rural to do with the country or farming

transcontinental crossing a continent

Index